Your Life As A Disciple

A 4-week course to help Chr [Christian]
teenagers develop a desire to serve
God

by Keith Drury

Group
Loveland, Colorado

Your Life as a Disciple
Copyright © 1990 by Group Publishing, Inc.

Sixth Printing, 1994

Credits
Edited by Stephen Parolini
Cover designed by Jill Bendykowski and DeWain Stoll
Interior designed by Judy Atwood Bienick and Jan Aufdemberge
Illustrations by Jan Aufdemberge and Judy Atwood Bienick
Cover photo by David Priest and Brenda Rundback
Photos on pp. 18, 41 and 42 by Jim Whitmer

ISBN 1-55945-204-8
Printed in the United States of America

CONTENTS

YOUR LIFE AS A DISCIPLE

Joslyn was a confused 10th-grader who hung around after every Sunday school class. She seemed to want to say something—but couldn't. After a few weeks, Joslyn finally told her teacher what had been on her mind.

"I don't think John and Stacy are real Christians."

"Why do you think that?" her teacher asked.

"Because, when they're not in church, they're out getting drunk or being cruel to other kids at school. They just don't act like Christians most of the time."

•••

How many of your teenagers "don't act like Christians"?

Some kids think they've got it made when they become Christians. They think they can go out and live however they want because they've already accepted Christ and received their "key" to God's kingdom.

Although their actions sometimes are to the contrary, teenagers do have specific expectations of what God expects of them as Christians. Check out the results of a survey of Christian teenagers below.

What Christian teenagers say God wants them to do:

84% ● To worship

82% ● To pray

82% ● To tell others about Jesus

77% ● To read the Bible

58% ● To do something about hunger, poverty and war

Christian teenagers seem to know what it means to be a Christian, but some have trouble putting that knowledge into practice. Many accept Jesus as their savior, only to find it's difficult to live each day as his disciple.

The church can help.

Teenagers can learn from the examples of the New Testament disciples how to live a lifestyle that's pleasing to God. And they can learn how to support one another and rely on God's help in order to live in obedient discipleship.

Your Life as a Disciple will help your teenagers understand what it means to be God's disciple. They'll learn how to live a consistent, exciting faith lifestyle.

HOW TO USE THIS COURSE

ACTIVE LEARNING

Think back on an important lesson you've learned in life. Did you learn it from reading about it? from hearing about it? from something you experienced? Chances are, the most important lessons you've learned came from something you experienced. That's what active learning is—learning by doing. And active learning is a key element in Group's Active Bible Curriculum.

Active learning leads students in doing things that help them understand important principles, messages and ideas. It's a discovery process that helps kids internalize what they learn.

Each lesson section in Group's Active Bible Curriculum plays an important part in active learning:

The **Opener** involves kids in the topic in fun and unusual ways.

The **Action and Reflection** includes an experience designed to evoke specific feelings in the students. This section also processes those feelings through "How did you feel?" questions and applies the message to situations kids face.

The **Bible Application** actively connects the topic with the Bible. It helps kids see how the Bible is relevant to the situations they face.

The **Commitment** helps students internalize the Bible's message and commit to make changes in their lives.

The **Closing** funnels the lesson's message into a time of creative reflection and prayer.

When you put all the sections together, you get a lesson that's fun to teach—and kids get messages they'll remember.

BEFORE THE 4-WEEK SESSION

● Read the Introduction, the Course Objectives and This Course at a Glance (p. 8).

● Decide how you'll publicize the course using the art on the Publicity Page (p. 9). Prepare fliers, newsletter articles and posters as needed.

● Look at the Bonus Ideas (p. 43) and decide which ones you'll use.

- Read the opening statements, Objectives and Bible Basis for the lesson. The Bible Basis shows how specific passages relate to senior highers today.
- Choose which Opener and Closing options to use. Each is appropriate for a different kind of group. The first option is often more active.
- Gather necessary supplies from This Lesson at a Glance.
- Read each section of the lesson. Adjust where necessary for your class size and meeting room.

- The approximate minutes listed give you an idea of how long each activity will take. Each lesson is designed to take 35 to 60 minutes. Shorten or lengthen activities as needed to fit your group.
- If you see you're going to have extra time, do an activity or two from the "If You Still Have Time . . ." box or from the Bonus Ideas (p. 43).
- Dive into the activities with the kids. Don't be a spectator. The lesson will be more successful and rewarding to both you and your students.

- The answers given after discussion questions are responses your students *might* give. They aren't the only answers or the "right" answers. If needed, use them to spark discussion. Kids won't always say what you wish they'd say. That's why some of the responses given are negative or controversial. If someone responds negatively, don't be shocked. Accept the person, and use the opportunity to explore other angles of the issue.

COURSE OBJECTIVES

By the end of this course your students will:
- become familiar with Jesus' original disciples;
- understand what discipleship is;
- understand what the Bible says about discipleship;
- explore what it means to be a disciple; and
- commit to developing a discipleship lifestyle.

THIS COURSE AT A GLANCE

Before you dive into the lessons, familiarize yourself with each lesson aim. Then read the scripture passages.
- Study them as a background to the lessons.
- Use them as a basis for your personal devotions.
- Think about how they relate to teenagers' circumstances today.

LESSON 1: TELL ME ABOUT THE JOB
Lesson Aim: To help senior highers learn about the first disciples and understand God's call to discipleship.
Bible Basis: Matthew 4:18-22 and John 1:43-49.

LESSON 2: WHAT ARE THE QUALIFICATIONS FOR DISCIPLESHIP?
Lesson Aim: To help senior highers understand what it means to be a disciple.
Bible Basis: Matthew 23:37; 26:40-41; and Luke 22:39-44.

LESSON 3: JOB-RELATED HAZARDS
Lesson Aim: To help senior highers understand and face the "cost" of discipleship.
Bible Basis: 2 Corinthians 11:23-29.

LESSON 4: YOU'VE GOT THE JOB!
Lesson Aim: To help senior highers become responsible disciples.
Bible Basis: Romans 12:9-21 and Matthew 28:16-20.

PUBLICITY PAGE

Grab your senior highers' attention! Copy this page, then cut and paste the art of your choice in your church bulletin or newsletter to advertise this course on discipleship. Or copy and use the ready-made flier as a bulletin insert.

Splash this art on posters, fliers or even postcards! Just add the vital details: the date and time the course begins, and where you'll meet.

It's that simple.

Your Life As **A Disciple**

Your Life As **A Disciple**

A 4-week senior high course on what it means to be a disciple

Come to _____

On _____

At _____

Come discover how you can live an exciting life as God's disciple!

your Life as a Disciple

Permission to photocopy this clip art granted for local church use. Copyright © Group Publishing, Inc., Box 481, Loveland, CO 80539.

TELL ME ABOUT THE JOB

Many teenagers think of "the disciples" as a dozen robed men who followed Jesus during his earthly ministry. It's easy to see the disciples as part of history—but it's not so easy to see how people can be disciples today. Teenagers need to understand that the first-century disciples can be models for disciples today.

To help senior highers learn about the first disciples and understand God's call to discipleship.

LESSON AIM

Students will:
- **examine some of the original disciples' lives;**
- **understand that God calls all people to discipleship;**
- **explore what it means to be a disciple; and**
- **evaluate their own discipleship.**

OBJECTIVES

Look up the following scriptures. Then read the background paragraphs to see how the passages relate to your senior highers.

BIBLE BASIS

MATTHEW 4:18-22
JOHN 1:43-49

In **Matthew 4:18-22**, Jesus calls Peter, Andrew, James and John to be his disciples.

Peter and Andrew were brothers in a fishing partnership with another set of brothers, James and John. They worked on the Sea of Galilee near Capernaum, which was to become Jesus' headquarters for his years of ministry. Though the fishing trade was not a wealthy profession, James and John were apparently men of decent means. Jesus called them to a deep level of commitment—following him full time.

Just as Jesus called these men to be his disciples, he calls each Christian to be his disciple. Teenagers need to understand that being a disciple is a full-time occupation.

In **John 1:43-49**, Jesus calls Philip and Nathanael to be his disciples.

Nathanael (also called Bartholomew) was from Cana, a town near Nazareth. Nazareth had a bad reputation from being a frequent stopping place for the Roman soldiers passing that way. It was, in a sense, a "party town." Prejudice against Nazareth was common in that day.

Just as Nathanael overcame his prejudice and decided to follow Jesus, teenagers need to leave their false perceptions behind and learn how to be Christ's disciples.

THIS LESSON AT A GLANCE

Section	Minutes	What Students Will Do	Supplies
Opener (Option 1)	5 to 10	**Connections**—Form groups and discover information about Jesus' disciples.	"Connections Cards" handouts (p. 17)
(Option 2)		**Job Wanted**—Look for jobs they like in classified ads.	Classified ads
Action and Reflection	10 to 15	**Least Likely**—Determine the least-likely candidate for discipleship.	Tape, newsprint, marker
Bible Application	10 to 15	**Real Disciples**—Read and talk about first-century disciples.	Bibles, newsprint, marker
Commitment	10 to 15	**Discipleship Inventory**—Complete a handout and reflect on their level of discipleship.	"Discipleship Inventory" handouts (p. 18), pencils
Closing (Option 1)	up to 5	**Discipleship Qualities**—Talk about qualities each person has that would make him or her a good disciple.	
(Option 2)		**Potential**—Share reasons why each person has great potential.	

The Lesson

OPENER
(5 to 10 minutes)

OPTION 1: CONNECTIONS
Copy and cut out the "Connections Cards" (p. 17). You'll need enough cards for each student to have one. For each "Find this disciple" card, there's a companion "You are a disciple" card. Be sure to include both cards of each set you distribute to teenagers. If you have more than 12 students, make additional copies of the cards. If you have fewer than

12 students, use only the number needed.

Fold the cards and mix them up. Then give one to each teenager. If you have an uneven number of students, give yourself a card and participate in the activity. Have kids each read their card. Then say: **If you have a "Find this disciple" card, go around and ask other people questions that'll help you find that person. You may only ask one question at a time of any one person. If you have a "You are a disciple" card, then answer questions asked by other students. After you find the person described on your card—or someone finds you—sit down.**

Remind students that some of the clues overlap. After all students have formed pairs, have the "finders" each introduce their "disciple" to the entire group.

Then ask:
● **What's a disciple?** (A person who followed Jesus in New Testament times; anyone who follows Jesus today; all Christians; a follower.)

Say: **A disciple is more than someone who lived during Jesus' day. Today we'll look at some of the original disciples and how Jesus calls us to be disciples too.**

OPTION 2: JOB WANTED

Form groups of no more than four. Give each group classified ads from recent newspapers.

Say: **Imagine for a moment you're a college graduate and looking for a job. Read the classified ads and find a job that appeals to you. Rip out that ad and tell your group what you might like about that job.**

Have groups each discuss and write down five things they can agree upon that they liked about the jobs they picked.

Ask:
● **What things did you like about these jobs?** (Good pay; nice company to work for; opportunity for promotion; location.)
● **What things made you avoid other jobs?** (Low pay; bad working conditions; low prestige job.)

Read aloud the "classified ads" in the margin.
Ask:
● **Which ad appeals to you most? Explain.** (The first, because it promises rewards; the second, because it offers great pay.)
● **Which ad appeals to you least? Explain.** (The first, because it sounds like a lot of work; the second, because it sounds too good to be true.)

Say: **If Jesus had placed an ad in the paper when he was looking for disciples, it probably would've sounded something like the first one. Just as you had a number of**

GREAT OPPORTUNITY for motivated worker who doesn't mind being in the minority. We promise hard work but good benefits for seasoned workers. Great company that quickly rewards highly motivated workers with responsibility.

GREAT OPPORTUNITY for person who likes being in the majority. High starting pay. High-risk opportunity with low effort. We promise lots of immediate rewards and an uncertain future. Join our massive company and enjoy an easy workload.

factors to consider in the newspaper ads you looked at, the disciples each had to consider the implications of becoming Jesus' disciple. We're going to see how a job description for Jesus' disciples might read today.

ACTION AND REFLECTION
(10 to 15 minutes)

LEAST LIKELY

Tape a sheet of newsprint to the wall. Say: **What might happen if Jesus came to our city and decided to call one or two students from your school as his disciples? Who would be the least-likely person in your school Jesus would call? Think about someone you think would make a terrible disciple.**

Tell teenagers not to mention any names. Have teenagers each call out descriptions of their person. List these qualities on the newsprint.

Have kids read over the list. Then say: **Imagine you're this person right now. And Jesus just walked in the room to call you to be his disciple.**

Ask:
● **How do you feel?** (Unworthy; uncomfortable; inadequate.)
● **Will you follow Jesus? Why or why not?** (Yes, he's hard to turn down; no, I don't feel worthy.)

Say: **Jesus didn't call disciples who were perfect. He called people who would follow him, learn from him and discover the wonders of God's kingdom.**

Write the following incomplete sentences, each on a separate sheet of newsprint, and tape them to the wall. Have teenagers complete the sentences verbally. Write their answers under the appropriate sentences.
● Jesus calls people to discipleship who . . . (Aren't perfect; are unlikely; have bad reputations.)
● The people Jesus calls to discipleship may feel . . . (Unworthy; afraid; angry; embarrassed; honored; happy.)
● Jesus chooses to call "ordinary" people to discipleship because . . . (They're more reliable; they respect his power; they're examples of his ability to change people.)

Say: **The job description for being a disciple doesn't require any formal training or skill. Even if you feel unworthy or inadequate, Jesus is interested in you. He can use any willing applicant.**

BIBLE APPLICATION
(10 to 15 minutes)

REAL DISCIPLES

Form groups no larger than six. Assign each group one of the following scripture passages:
● Matthew 4:18-22   ● Matthew 19:16-22
● Matthew 9:9-13   ● John 1:43-49

Have groups each read aloud and talk about their scripture. Write the following questions on newsprint. Then have groups discuss the questions.

● How did Jesus deal with the people in this scripture? What did he say? do? Explain.

● How might the person Jesus dealt with have felt in this situation?

● What were the results of Jesus' dealings with this person?

Have someone from each group share the group's discoveries with the rest of the groups. Then have teenagers each talk about which disciple they feel most like.

Ask:

● **What does it mean to be called to be a disciple?** (To serve God daily; to have a close relationship with God.)

DISCIPLESHIP INVENTORY

Give each student a copy of the "Discipleship Inventory" handout (p. 18) and a pencil. Say: **Jesus has called all Christians to discipleship. This inventory is just between God and you; nobody will ask you to share what you've written. Think about your response to Christ's call to commitment as you answer the questions.**

When the handouts are completed, have students each fold theirs and put it in their Bible or pocket. Form groups of no more than four and have kids talk about how they felt about their inventories. Then have groups pause for silent prayer. Encourage teenagers to reflect on how they can be better disciples.

OPTION 1: DISCIPLESHIP QUALITIES

Form pairs. Have kids briefly describe how they feel about being called to discipleship. Then have them each tell one or two positive discipleship qualities their partner has. Form a circle with all the students and close by singing a familiar song.

OPTION 2: POTENTIAL

Form groups of no more than four. Have groups each sit in a circle. Say: **Just like the first-century disciples, most of us don't feel up to the call to deeper discipleship. However, Jesus sees our potential—he believes in us. And we believe in each other. Have you ever noticed how it's often easier to believe in someone else's potential than to believe in your own?**

Have each student confess one area where he or she feels inadequate, uncertain or fearful. Then have kids each make an affirming or encouraging statement about the future potential of the person to their right.

COMMITMENT
(10 to 15 minutes)

CLOSING
(up to 5 minutes)

If You Still Have Time . . .

Discipleship Acrostic—Form groups of no more than three. Give each group a sheet of newsprint and markers. Have the groups each make an acrostic for the word "discipleship" with each letter representing a word or phrase descriptive of what it means to be a disciple. Bring groups back together to share their results.

Disciple Limericks—Form groups of no more than four, and see which group can come up with the best limerick or poem describing one of the Bible disciples. Then have groups each share their creation. Make this a fun, low-pressure activity.

A limerick is a five-line poem—usually silly—where the first two lines and the last line rhyme, and the third and fourth line rhyme. Here are examples to get your groups started:

> There once was a fellow named Matt,
> whose pockets of gold were right fat.
> > Then the Lord came along,
> > and Matt felt he'd been wrong
> so he got up and left where he'd sat.

> A guy named Nathanael once said,
> In Nazareth I wouldn't be caught dead.
> > Then along came the Son,
> > Who was "A"-number one,
> and ol' Nat from then on was led.

CONNECTIONS CARDS

Find this disciple:
1. He's a fisherman in business with his brother and two others.
2. He used to be John the Baptist's disciple.

You are a discple.
You have a fishing business with your brother, Peter, and two others. You used to follow John the Baptist until Jesus came along. Now you follow Jesus. Your name is ANDREW.

Find this disciple:
1. He's a fisherman in business with his brother and two others.
2. He likes to talk a lot; he's a natural leader.

You are a disciple.
You have a fishing business with your brother, Andrew, and partners, James and John. You love to talk and always seem to be the leader of groups you're in. Your name is SIMON, but Jesus changed it to PETER.

Find this disciple:
1. He wrote one of the four Gospels in the Bible.
2. Jesus' nickname for him and his brother is "Sons of Thunder."

You are a disciple.
You're the author of one of the Gospels. Jesus nicknamed you and your brother the "Sons of Thunder" because of your hot tempers. Your name is JOHN.

Find this disciple:
1. Jesus' nickname for him and his brother is "Sons of Thunder."
2. His brother is often called "The Apostle of Love."

You are a disciple.
Jesus nicknamed you and your brother the "Sons of Thunder" because of your hot tempers. Your brother is known as "The Apostle of Love." Your name is JAMES.

Find this disciple:
1. He's a quiet and shy person.
2. He's a practical, calculating man—even figuring out how much it would cost to feed a crowd.

You are a disciple.
You're a shy man, not inclined to be in the spotlight. You like numbers and calculating—even figuring out things like how much it would cost to feed a crowd. Your name is PHILIP.

Find this disciple:
1. He's from the city of Cana near Nazareth.
2. He was brought to Jesus by his friend Philip.

You are a disciple.
You live in the city of Cana, where Jesus turned the water into wine. Your friend Philip brought you to Jesus. Your name is NATHANAEL.

Discipleship
I N V E N T O R Y

Check an answer that best represents your response to Jesus' call to discipleship—or write in your own answer.

1. Which of the following best represents my level of commitment to Christ?
___I'm a "maximum Christian"—fully committed to Christ.
___I'm an average follower—neither hot nor cold.
___I'm a follower, but not very serious about it.
___I'm near to becoming a follower, but haven't yet chosen Christ.
___I'm not the least bit interested in becoming a follower.
___ (My own answer) _____.

2. When I think God wants me to really get serious in discipleship, I feel:
___Unworthy. I'm not good enough to be a real disciple.
___Scared. I'm afraid of what true discipleship might require.
___Challenged. I want to be the best disciple I can be.
___Unwilling. I don't like what discipleship involves.
___Uncertain. I don't know what it all means.
___(My own answer) _____.

3. Things that hold me back from deeper discipleship might include:
___How my friends would react.
___How my parents would react.
___Past things I've done that I'm not proud of.
___Lack of time to invest in becoming a serious disciple.
___The hypocrisy I see in other so-called disciples in the church.
___(My own answer) _____.

4. One single action I'd be willing to take this week to begin moving toward deeper discipleship is:

WHAT ARE THE QUALIFICATIONS FOR DISCIPLESHIP?

Discipleship isn't something people automatically receive when they become Christians. Teenagers need to learn that it takes discipline and a willing attitude to be Jesus' disciple.

To help senior highers understand what it means to be a disciple.

Students will:
● **experience the difficulty of leading the unwilling;**
● **explore what the Bible teaches about a willing spirit; and**
● **examine their own attitude of willingness.**

Look up the following scriptures. Then read the background paragraphs to see how the passages relate to your senior highers.

In **Matthew 23:37**, Jesus speaks out against Jerusalem. Jesus was nearing the end of his ministry on Earth—the cross was not far away. He had just spoken to the Pharisees. He wrapped up his condemnation of the Pharisees' hypocritical behavior with an aching summary about the city of cities—Jerusalem. You can almost imagine his sad expression as he says, "you were not willing."

Teenagers can sometimes be stubborn like the Pharisees. They don't want to change old habits because the risks are "too great." But Jesus wants teenagers to be willing to serve God. And once teenagers put on an "attitude of willingness," they'll begin to see how God can use them.

In **Matthew 26:40-41**, Jesus confronts his disciples about sleeping while he prays in Gethsemane.

Jesus and his disciples were already tired when they went to the garden of Gethsemane for an "all-nighter." Jesus observed that the spirit—our desire—may at times be willing yet the body or flesh may be weak.

Teenagers can easily relate to the disciples' struggles. They may want to obey God but find it difficult to actually follow through with their desire.

In **Luke 22:39-44**, Jesus prays in Gethsemane for God's will to be done.

Jesus' prayer in this passage is a dynamic reminder of always asking for God's will to be done even when it might mean pain or suffering.

One of the most difficult prayers to pray is "Not my will but yours be done." But the road to discipleship includes learning how to accept God's will. It's a challenge teenagers—and all Christians—must face.

THIS LESSON AT A GLANCE

Section	Minutes	What Students Will Do	Supplies
Opener (Option 1)	5 to 10	**Frustration Game**—Discover the difficulty of getting people to do something when they're unwilling.	
(Option 2)		**Unwillingness Stories**—Share personal experiences when they've been willing.	
Action and Reflection	10 to 15	**Wall-Street Trader**—Learn how quickly something can be done if people are willing.	"Shares" cards (p. 25), paper, scissors
Bible Application	10 to 15	**Willingness**—Study Bible passages about willingness.	Bibles, copies of "Read and Think" box (p. 23), scissors
Commitment	10 to 15	**Willing Spirit Ballot**—Examine their willingness level and commit to being disciples.	"Willing Spirit Ballot" handouts (p. 26), pencils
Closing (Option 1)	up to 5	**Willing to Be Willing**—Participate in a candlelight worship service.	Candles, matches
(Option 2)		**Willing Huddle**—Participate in a group hug.	Bible

The Lesson

OPTION 1: FRUSTRATION GAME

Before starting this activity, read the instructions and the "Before the Class" box in the margin. Form two groups and choose a volunteer from each group to be an "interview guest" for a press conference. Have the interview guests leave the room with an escort. Then explain that the contest is to see which group can first get its interview guest to say the word "school." Say: **Get your interview guest to say "school" without saying it yourself. Ask questions that lead your guest to use "school" in the answers. As soon as your guest says "school," applaud loudly.**

Bring the interview guests in and seat them behind a table. Introduce the guests with something like: **We're delighted to have with us two of the most famous students in our area. Today we're going to find out their secrets for success.**

Have groups alternate asking questions of their interview guests. After each group has asked five questions, stop the interviews and tell everyone about the instructions given to the interview guests.

Ask:

● **How did you feel when you couldn't get your guest to say "school"?** (Frustrated; angry; like giving up; suspicious.)

● **How did the guests feel knowing what the groups were after?** (Guilty; powerful.)

● **Why is it hard to get someone to do or say something they don't want to do or say?** (People don't like to be told what to do; people have a free will.)

● **How are we sometimes like the interview guests when God wants us to do or say something?** (We know but won't listen; we feel powerful saying no.)

Say: **A willing heart is one of the primary qualifications for being God's disciple. We're going to look at what it takes to have a willing heart in discipleship.**

OPTION 2: UNWILLINGNESS STORIES

Open the lesson by telling a personal anecdote about when you were unwilling to do something. It might be something your parents, a teacher, a coach or a friend wanted you to do. Then form groups of no more than five.

Say: **In your groups, take turns sharing a time in the**

OPENER
(5 to 10 minutes)

Before the Class

Choose a class member to be an escort for this activity. Secretly prompt the escort to explain the following to the two interview guests: **You'll be interviewed by your group. Answer questions any way you want. Kids will be trying to get you to say the word "school." Avoid the word "school" no matter what. Say "classes," the name of your school, names of teachers, anything else—just don't say "school." Also don't let them find out you know they're after the word "school."**

past or present when you've been unwilling to do or say something someone else was trying to get you to say or do.

Allow four or five minutes for teenagers to share their stories. Go from group to group to help prompt discussion. If kids don't immediately jump at the chance to do this activity, use that unwillingness to spark whole-group discussion on the subject.

Form a circle.

Ask:

● **How do you think others felt when they wanted you to do something but you didn't want to do it?** (Angry; frustrated; concerned.)

● **How do you think God feels when we're unwilling to do his work?** (Angry; sad; frustrated.)

Say: **Unwillingness is probably something God deals with a lot. Even Jesus' first disciples struggled to do God's will from time to time. But the key to successful discipleship is a willing attitude. Today we'll look at what it means to have a willing attitude.**

ACTION AND REFLECTION
(10 to 15 minutes)

WALL-STREET TRADER

Make copies of the "Shares" cards (p. 25) and cut them apart. Be sure to have 10 of each kind and one kind of "stock" for each person in the class. Shuffle the cards and form piles of 10 cards each.

Say: **For this game, we're going to pretend we're on the floor of the New York Stock Exchange. The object of the game is to corner the market on any one kind of stock—that is, collect each share representing a certain kind of stock. Each of you will start with 10 shares of stock—but they'll be from different companies. Your job is to get 10 shares of stock exactly alike.**

When you collect all 10 shares of a stock, come up to me so I can record your names in the order you finish. The way to trade is to shout out what stock you're trading or looking for until you find someone to trade with. Trade away the exact number of shares you receive each time. One for one, two for two, and so on. The faster you trade, the quicker you'll get a full set.

Distribute a shuffled pile of 10 shares to each player. Then announce: **The market is open.**

As teenagers each get a corner on a stock, write their name on the piece of paper and watch how quickly the rest finish.

After the game, ask:

● **What made getting a corner on the market hard for you?** (Other people were going for the same stock; some people wouldn't trade.)

● **What made it easy for you?** (I had a lot of one kind of stock to begin with; everyone was willing to trade.)

● **How would've it turned out if one person had refused**

to trade? (No one would've won; it would've taken a while to find a winner.)

● **How did everyone help everyone else?** (Gave what they had in order to get what they wanted; they didn't help each other.)

● **In what way is this game like being a Christian?** (Each person has something to give; people must be willing to give in order to benefit; if everyone is willing to give, all benefit.)

Say: **Discipleship begins with a willingness to give of yourself. As we learned in the game, nothing was accomplished unless people were willing to give. That's true, too, of being a disciple. Even Jesus' disciples struggled with their attitudes of willingness. Next we'll look at how their struggles can help us become more willing to give of ourselves.**

WILLINGNESS

Form groups of no more than six. Copy and cut apart the "Read and Think" box. Give a different "Read and Think" section and a Bible to each group. Have groups each read their scripture and discuss the questions.

BIBLE APPLICATION
(10 to 15 minutes)

Read and Think

Passage: **Matthew 23:37**

Answer these questions:
- Who's speaking here? Who is he speaking about?
- Who are the children he's referring to?
- How does our willingness (or lack of willingness) to serve God affect what God can do in and through us?

- -

Passage: **Matthew 26:40-41**

Answer these questions:
- Where did this story take place?
- When in Christ's ministry did this occur?
- Why did the disciples go to sleep?
- What temptation was Jesus speaking of?
- What two parts of a person did Jesus refer to here? What's the difference between the willingness of body and spirit?
- What does this passage tell us about willingness?

- -

Passage: **Luke 22:39-44**

Answer these questions:
- Where did this story take place? When?
- What was Jesus' prayer request to God?
- What's the meaning of verse 42?
- Why was Jesus in such anguish?
- How should we pray when we think what we want isn't what God wants?

Allow about 10 minutes, then gather everyone together. Have several students share discoveries from their study.

Say: **As we can see from the Bible passages, a willing heart isn't always easy—but it's important. Jesus best demonstrated this when he prayed "not my will, but yours be done" as he faced the pain of the cross.**

COMMITMENT
(10 to 15 minutes)

WILLING SPIRIT BALLOT

Distribute a "Willing Spirit Ballot" (p. 26) and a pencil to each student. Say: **We've seen how important willingness is in discipleship. One thing you can count on about God—he won't make you a disciple against your will. In fact, there's just one qualification for the job of discipleship—willingness to do God's work.**

Have teenagers each find a quiet place in the room to read and complete the "Willing Spirit Ballot." Then have them form pairs. Have kids each encourage their partner to have a willing spirit by saying: "(Name), I challenge you to let God use your talents and abilities." Then have them each tell why they think their partner would make a good disciple.

CLOSING
(up to 5 minutes)

OPTION 1: WILLING TO BE WILLING

Light six or more candles on a table. After partners finish encouraging each other, have them quietly kneel in a circle around the table. When the entire group is assembled, start humming a familiar song. Invite students to hum along. Have someone turn out the lights.

In a quiet voice, say: **We've been talking about willingness—being willing to let God make disciples of us. As we close, let's pray silently for willing attitudes.**

After a moment of silent prayer, have teenagers blow out the candles and sit silently for a few seconds. Remind kids this is a time of worship and serious reflection.

OPTION 2: WILLING HUDDLE

Form a circle and have teenagers place their arms around each other to form a group hug. Read aloud Psalm 51:12.

Say: **As we close in prayer, I want each of you to pray silently for the person to your right. Pray that God will develop in him or her this willing attitude. After you've prayed for the person on your right, say "Amen" aloud.**

If You Still Have Time . . .

More Wall Street—Play additional rounds of the Wall-Street Trader game. Have teenagers talk about how the game reflects how people work together in real life.

Strong-Willed Students—Form groups of no more than four. Have teenagers each share areas in their life where they're strong-willed—things they won't eat, places they won't go, activities they simply won't do. Have teenagers talk about the positive and negative aspects of strong-willed attitudes.

Copy and cut apart the following share cards. If you have more than 12 students in your class, add some of your own in the space provided.

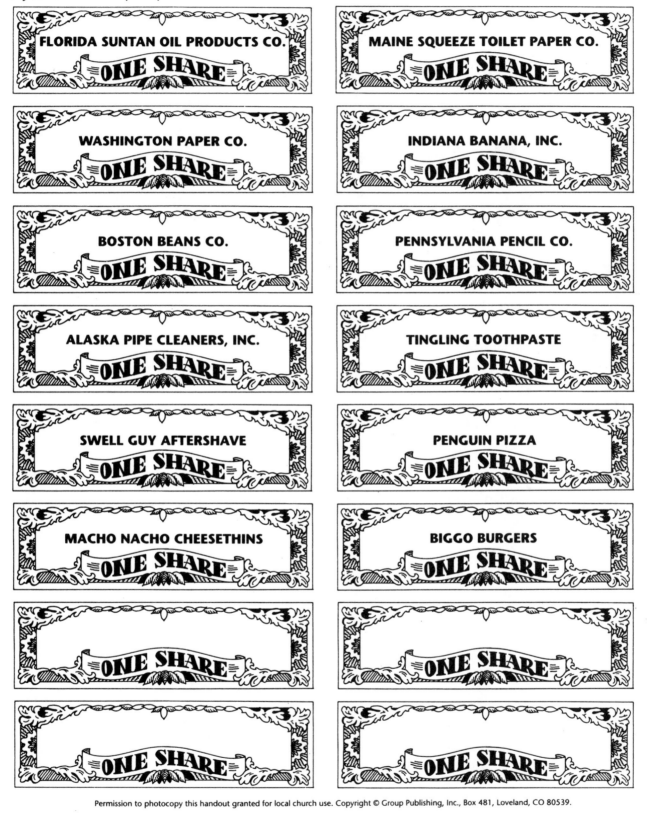

FLORIDA SUNTAN OIL PRODUCTS CO.
ONE SHARE

MAINE SQUEEZE TOILET PAPER CO.
ONE SHARE

WASHINGTON PAPER CO.
ONE SHARE

INDIANA BANANA, INC.
ONE SHARE

BOSTON BEANS CO.
ONE SHARE

PENNSYLVANIA PENCIL CO.
ONE SHARE

ALASKA PIPE CLEANERS, INC.
ONE SHARE

TINGLING TOOTHPASTE
ONE SHARE

SWELL GUY AFTERSHAVE
ONE SHARE

PENGUIN PIZZA
ONE SHARE

MACHO NACHO CHEESETHINS
ONE SHARE

BIGGO BURGERS
ONE SHARE

ONE SHARE

ONE SHARE

ONE SHARE

ONE SHARE

WILLING SPIRIT BALLOT

Read each statement carefully. Then place a checkmark next to each statement you agree with. After completing the ballot, take a moment to think about how you can develop a willing spirit.

☐ I'm willing to become a follower of Christ.

☐ I'm willing to let God change what needs to be changed in my life.

☐ I'm willing to make specific changes in my life to be a better disciple.

☐ I'm willing to stop activities or attitudes that keep me from being a disciple.

☐ I'm willing to risk people picking on me and laughing at me to be the best disciple I can be.

JOB-RELATED HAZARDS

Christians are persecuted, ignored and avoided because of their discipleship lifestyle. Teenagers need to understand the risks involved in discipleship—and that they're not left alone to face these "job-related hazards."

To help senior highers understand and face the "cost" of discipleship.

LESSON AIM

Students will:
- **experience risks and the rewards of risks;**
- **explore what it cost some first-century Christians to be disciples; and**
- **reflect on the rewards of discipleship.**

OBJECTIVES

Look up the following scripture. Then read the background paragraphs to see how the passage relates to your senior highers.

BIBLE BASIS
2 CORINTHIANS 11:23-29

In **2 Corinthians 11:23-29**, Paul tells about his sufferings. Throughout Paul's ministry he experienced a variety of difficulties, many of which are recorded in the book of Acts. In this 2 Corinthians passage, Paul lists experiences that go beyond Luke's record in Acts. All disciples experienced hardships during the first century, but we know more about Paul's life. He was persecuted by the Jewish leaders, the Roman government and the conservative Christians. And he often dealt with the trials of travel—especially boat travel.

Teenagers who want to be real disciples face similar tough situations. Friends at school may taunt or tease them, parents may ridicule them and even other Christians may look down on them. But, like Paul, they can learn to overcome the difficulties and continue to develop a discipleship lifestyle—no matter the cost.

Section	Minutes	What Students Will Do	Supplies
Opener (Option 1) (Option 2)	5 to 10	**Danger Is My Name**—Have a volunteer recruit people for dangerous jobs. **Most Dangerous Time**—Talk about dangerous things they've done.	Copies of "Profile and Job Openings" box (p. 29)
Action and Reflection	15 to 20	**Take a Risk**—Experience how it feels to take a risk.	Blindfolds, prizes
Bible Application	10 to 15	**Hazardous Duty**—Complete a handout and discuss risks of discipleship.	"Hazardous Duty Warning" handouts (p. 33), pencils, Bibles
Commitment	5 to 10	**Risks and Rewards**—List risks and rewards of discipleship.	3×5 cards, pencils, cassette of soft music, cassette player, wooden cross
Closing (Option 1) (Option 2)	up to 5	**Prices I've Paid**—Talk about times they've "paid a price" for their belief in Christ. **Shared Cost**—Talk about how they can support each other in discipleship.	Coins, buckets or large cups

The Lesson

OPENER
(5 to 10 minutes)

OPTION 1: DANGER IS MY NAME

Talk with a teenager ahead of time to play the role of Duke or Diane Danger, the owner and president of Dangerous Jobs International. Or you may wish to play the role yourself. Give Duke or Diane a copy of the "Profile and Job Openings" box. Have him or her read it and follow the instructions.

Announce that a special guest from Dangerous Jobs International has come to interview candidates for placement in hazardous positions around the world.

After Duke or Diane finishes "recruiting" teenagers, ask:

● **Why would people want to do this kind of work?** (They like the money; they enjoy danger.)

● **What would keep people from applying for this kind of work?** (It's dangerous; they'd be afraid they might fail.)

● **How are these dangerous jobs sometimes like being a disciple?**

● **What are the dangers associated with each job?** (Injury; death; pain.)

● **What are the dangers associated with being a disci-ple?** (Rejection; persecution; being laughed at.)

Profile and Job Openings

Duke or Diane Danger

Owner and president: Dangerous Jobs International

You travel across the country to recruit teenagers for dangerous jobs worldwide. You're not afraid of danger. In fact, you live for danger.

Introduce yourself to the class. Then describe your company, and tell the students about one or two of your dangerous assignments—like the time you were in Africa, surrounded by 50 hungry lions . . .

Then explain the following job openings. Do your best to convince kids to sign up for one of these jobs:

● **Wanted: "Hellfire Fighters"** to put out oil-rig fires by exploding dynamite near the fire. People must be good swimmers, agile and very fast. Pay: $150,000 per fire—plus funeral expenses if needed.

● **Wanted: Mercenary Soldiers** to fight guerrilla soldiers for a South American dictatorship. People must be proficient in use of firearms, skilled in ambush work and understand the value of good life insurance. Pay: $500 a week and a $50,000 bonus for each year you stay alive.

● **Wanted: Chemical-Waste-Disposal Workers** to package, transport and dispose of dangerous chemical waste. People must be able to lift 50-pound barrels and carry their own cancer insurance. Pay: $1,000 a week plus all the toxic waste you'll ever need.

Say: **Discipleship is a risky venture. Once you've become a willing disciple, the next step is to understand and accept the cost of discipleship.**

OPTION 2: MOST DANGEROUS TIME

Form groups of no more than six. Ask teenagers each to share with their group the "most dangerous situation I was ever in." Then form a circle with the whole group.

Ask:

● **Did any of you experience danger because of circumstances beyond your control? Explain.**

● **Did any of you purposely do something dangerous? Explain.**

● **What makes danger worth the risk?** (A reward; the thrill of danger.)

Say: **Risk is a major aspect of being a disciple. Today we're going to look at how the risks and rewards balance in discipleship.**

TAKE A RISK

Quickly set up a Risk Route obstacle course. Arrange tables and chairs to create a complicated and dangerously difficult course. Blindfold two or three volunteers. Have every-

ACTION AND REFLECTION

(15 to 20 minutes)

one else stand around the course in a crowded circle. Then move the tables and chairs around noisily—but place them back where they were to begin with before sending the volunteers through the course.

Select a student guide to guide the volunteers through the course by voice instructions. Have the group respond to the volunteers' immediate circumstances by offering gasps, warnings and applause to enhance the atmosphere of danger. After students finish the course, have everyone applaud. Repeat the activity a few times with different volunteers. Each time, rearrange the tables and chairs to create new courses. Then award prizes—fruit, doughnuts or candy bars—to the people who made it through the course.

Ask the volunteers:

● **How did you feel going through the course? Explain.** (Scared, I didn't know what I might run into; cautious, I didn't want to fall down.)

● **Did you think we were tricking you when you heard the chairs and tables move? Explain.** (Yes, I thought you were making the course harder.)

● **How did you feel about your guide?** (I trusted him or her; I felt nervous.)

● **How did the group's comments make you feel?** (Confused; upset.)

● **How did you feel about the reward?** (Good; happy; satisfied.)

Ask the rest of the students:

● **How did you see the danger differently from the volunteers?** (Didn't seem difficult to us; we could see.)

● **What did you think when the volunteers received their reward?** (I wished I'd done the course; it wasn't fair.)

Say: **The risks of discipleship are like the risks of the Risk Route. You don't always know what's coming up or what obstacles you'll face—but the reward of a closer relationship with God is always waiting at the other end of the risk. And while the Risk Route award lasts only a short time, your improved relationship with God can last a lifetime.**

BIBLE APPLICATION
(10 to 15 minutes)

HAZARDOUS DUTY

Form groups of no more than four. Give groups each a "Hazardous Duty Warning" handout (p. 33), a pencil and a Bible. Tell each group they're the Dangerous Duty Committee. Have students work together to complete the handout. Then have groups each present their findings to the rest of the kids in a creative way. Suggest they might create a rap, poem, skit or song to describe the risks listed in the completed handout.

Form one group and ask:

● **Why would the first disciples take these risks?** (Out of love for God; for the reward of heaven.)

● **How do you think the disciples might have felt at the**

time? (Like giving up; tired; depressed.)

● **What would make someone today take such risks?** (A reward; love for God.)

● **How do you feel when you face situations that test your faith?** (Angry; tired; depressed.)

Say: **The cost of discipleship is sometimes great. You may be laughed at, ignored or even verbally or physically abused. But the reward of a closer relationship to God is worth the pain and humiliation.**

RISKS AND REWARDS

Distribute a 3×5 card and a pencil to each student. Have soft music playing. Place a cross on a table.

Say: **This part of the lesson is between you and God—no one will ask you to tell what you write on your card—so don't sign your name. Across the top of one side of your card write "Rewards." Then list one or two rewards you get for being a serious disciple.** (Pause) **Now across the top of the other side of the card write "Risks." List one or two things you're willing to risk to gain the rewards listed on the other side.** (Pause) **Jesus never promised us easy discipleship, but he did promise that the cost would be worth the pain or humiliation we might feel.**

As the music continues to play, invite students each to show their willingness to risk for Jesus' sake by placing their card face down on a table with a cross on it.

Say: **Just as we place these cards on this table, we place our lives in God's hands. Let this moment be a time of commitment for each of us as we boldly step forward to face the cost of discipleship.**

OPTION 1: PRICES I'VE PAID

Form groups of six or fewer. Have groups each form a circle. Give kids each a coin—a penny, nickel, dime or quarter. Place a bucket or large cup in the center of each circle. Have teenagers each share one time they "paid a price" for their belief in Christ. Tell kids it's okay to be silent. After each person's turn, have him or her drop the coin into the bucket. Then have the rest of the kids in the circle say why they appreciate that person's willingness to be a disciple.

Have each group close in a time of silent prayer. Then have teenagers go around and challenge each other to be willing to risk for Jesus' sake by saying: "(Name), go out and be a bold disciple. With God's help, I know you can do it."

OPTION 2: SHARED COST

Have teenagers stand in a circle and hold hands. Then say: **Being a disciple is difficult when people give you a hard time. But when disciples band together, they learn to sup-**

COMMITMENT
(5 to 10 minutes)

CLOSING
(up to 5 minutes)

port each other when dangers arise.

Have teenagers each say specific things they can do to support the person on their left. After going around the circle, have kids say together: "Let us share the cost of discipleship as we seek to serve God." Have a volunteer close in prayer.

If You Still Have Time . . .

It's Worth It!—Form groups of no more than five and have groups each create a poster based on the theme "It's hard to be a disciple, but it's worth it!" Suggest they use Hebrews 11:32-40 and 12:1 as the basis for the posters.

Risky Business—Form pairs. Have partners talk about times they took risks. Encourage teenagers to talk about how they felt about the risks and rewards in those situations. Then have them talk about what it must have been like to be one of Jesus' disciples after his Ascension into heaven.

Hazardous Duty
WARNING

Read the following scripture passages: 2 Corinthians 11:23-29; Acts 6:8-15; 7:54—8:3; and 12:1-11. Then based on what you read, list risks associated with being a disciple.

WARNING: The Dangerous Duty Committee has determined that discipleship may be considered hazardous work.

LESSON 4

YOU'VE GOT THE JOB!

Teenagers may understand the qualifications for discipleship and even the hazards or risks of discipleship. But *understanding* what it means to be a disciple isn't the same as *being* a disciple. Teenagers may need encouragement and support to become serious disciples.

LESSON AIM

To help senior highers become responsible disciples.

OBJECTIVES

Students will:
- **understand the nature of the Great Commission;**
- **examine characteristics of a discipleship lifestyle; and**
- **commit to develop a specific discipleship characteristic.**

BIBLE BASIS

ROMANS 12:9-21
MATTHEW 28:16-20

Look up the following scriptures. Then read the background paragraphs to see how the passages relate to your senior highers.

In **Romans 12:9-21**, Paul gives guidelines for relating to society.

This passage describes the practical life a disciple of Christ is urged to live. In the first 11 chapters of Romans, Paul traces how God reaches out to people. But in chapter 12, he begins challenging people to respond to God's call for discipleship. Paul wants people to be committed to serving God.

Teenagers live in a society where commitment is rare. But commitment is the key to a discipleship lifestyle.

Discipleship isn't a temporary or part-time job. It's a way of life and requires people to stretch and grow as they seek and live God's will.

In **Matthew 28:16-20**, Jesus tells his disciples to go and make disciples of all the nations.

In this passage, often referred to as the Great Commission, Jesus tells his disciples to seek out, teach and baptize people all around the world. His command is accompanied by more than a simple wish for success; Jesus promises he'll be with his disciples as they reach out to the people.

Christians are called to be Christ's disciples. But many teenagers feel unprepared to seek out, teach and baptize people. Jesus' promise to be with them can help teenagers realize they can call upon God's strength as they do his work.

THIS LESSON AT A GLANCE

Section	Minutes	What Students Will Do	Supplies
Opener (Option 1)	5 to 10	**Choose Me**—Form a human sculpture and talk about how it feels to be chosen for something.	Camera (optional)
(Option 2)		**You Already Work Here**—Discuss a role play involving a job applicant and an interviewer.	
Action and Reflection	10 to 15	**Job Description**—Complete a handout and talk about what it means to accept the job of disciple.	"Job Description" hand-outs (p. 40), pencils
Bible Application	10 to 15	**Discipleship Lifestyle**—Complete a handout examining the characteristics of a discipleship lifestyle.	"Discipleship Lifestyle" (p. 41), pencils, Bibles
Commitment	10 to 15	**Sign on the Dotted Line**—Commit to developing a specific discipleship characteristic.	Paper, pencils, candles, matches, "Discipleship Lifestyle" handouts from Discipleship Lifestyle.
Closing (Option 1)	up to 5	**Prayer Circle**—Pray for each other.	Papers from Sign on the Dotted Line
(Option 2)		**Discipleship Sentences**—Complete sentences about how they feel about discipleship.	Papers from Sign on the Dotted Line

The Lesson

OPTION 1: CHOOSE ME

Create an unusual human sculpture with all your students. But don't tell them what you'll be doing. Say: **Today, we're going to open our lesson with a special activity. I'll need a few helpers for this activity.**

OPENER
(5 to 10 minutes)

Choose two or three teenagers from your class. Arrange them in unusual positions in front of the class. Use books, chairs and tables to make the human sculpture more interesting. As you position each person, pretend you have a specific plan for the completed sculpture—even if you don't. After the first students are locked into position, choose a few more students. Do this until all kids are part of the sculpture. Be creative as you arrange the teenagers.

When the sculpture is complete, say: **There, now we've got it.**

Pull out a camera if you brought one, and take a picture of the strange sculpture. Encourage teenagers to look around at the sculpture and then have them sit in a circle.

Ask:

● **What did you think we were going to do?** (A skit; a trick; I don't know.)

● **What were you thinking as I kept picking students to help with the activity?** (How many more would be picked; what's the activity?)

● **How did you feel when you were chosen to help out?** (Nervous; glad; embarrassed.)

● **How did you feel when I put you in unusual positions?** (Uncomfortable; nervous.)

● **How is being picked to participate in this activity like being called to discipleship?** (Everyone is called; being called to discipleship can make you uncomfortable or nervous.)

Say: **We're all called to discipleship. And we may feel uncomfortable or uneasy about the "job" of discipleship. Today we'll take a look at how we can boldly accept the job and move forward as Christ's disciples.**

Applicant

You're trying to get a job as head counselor at Saddle Lake Camp this summer. Try to impress the interviewer with your qualifications: how good you are with kids, your good grades at school, your interest in sports and how hard you'll work. The interviewer will keep interrupting to tell you you've already got the job. Ignore this and keep telling—even repeating—your qualifications in order to convince him or her to hire you.

Interviewer

Your job is easy. The applicant is trying to get a job at the summer camp you operate. You've already decided to hire this applicant so hearing all about his or her qualifications is irrelevant. Keep interrupting the applicant to say "but you've already got the job." The applicant will ignore you, but keep telling this person he or she has already been hired.

OPTION 2: YOU ALREADY WORK HERE

Choose two teenagers for a brief role play. Have one read the Applicant box and the other read the Interviewer box in the margin. Then have the participants play out the scene for no more than two minutes.

After the role play, ask:

● **What was the applicant trying to do in this role play?** (Get a job he or she already had; convince the interviewer he or she was qualified for the job.)

● **How did you feel when the applicant kept on talking after the job was already his or hers?** (Annoyed; frustrated.)

● **How do you think an interviewer would feel in this situation?** (Frustrated; irritated.)

Say: **In this situation, the applicant for the job didn't listen to the interviewer. When we consider our call to discipleship, we may act like the applicant in this role play. Even though we've already been given the job of disciple, we may not hear God's call. Sometimes we're too busy explaining why we are or aren't the best person for the job rather than accepting the call and beginning work. We're going to examine the importance of taking the job of disciple and living a discipleship lifestyle.**

Table Talk

The Table Talk activity in this course helps senior highers discuss the meaning of discipleship with their parents.

If you choose to use the Table Talk activity, this is a good time to show students the "Table Talk" handout (p. 42). Ask them to spend time with their parents completing it.

Before kids leave, give them each the "Table Talk" handout to take home or tell them you'll be sending it to their parents.

Or use the Table Talk idea found in the Bonus Ideas (p. 44) for a meeting based on the handout.

JOB DESCRIPTION

Form groups of no more than five. Distribute a "Job Description" handout (p. 40) and a pencil to each group. Have groups each complete the handout. Give groups five to seven minutes to complete the handout.

Gather everyone together, and have representatives from each group report on how they completed the "Job Description" handout.

Ask:

● **What common elements are in all your job descriptions?** (The job's not easy; the benefits are great.)

● **If you'd never heard of discipleship and read these descriptions for the first time, would you take the job? Why or why not?** (Yes, the benefits seem pretty good; no, the negatives are too great.)

● **What are your responsibilities when you accept a job?** (To do the job asked of you; try your best to do the work.)

● **What are your responsibilities when you accept a job to be Christ's disciple?** (To do the job well; to do your best to be a good disciple.)

Say: **We've already talked about the qualifications for being a disciple, the job-related hazards and the job description. Next we're going to read suggestions from the Bible on how to do the job well.**

ACTION AND REFLECTION
(10 to 15 minutes)

DISCIPLESHIP LIFESTYLE

Form groups of no more than four. Distribute a "Discipleship Lifestyle" handout (p. 41) and a pencil to each teenager. Give each group a Bible. Have someone in each group read aloud Romans 12:9-21. Then have teenagers each complete the handout and discuss it in their group. Then have them read Matthew 28:16-20. Have them discuss what this passage means for them.

After groups have briefly discussed the handouts, gather everyone together. Ask teenagers to share examples of how to exhibit each of the characteristics listed on the handout. For example, someone might say, "In order to live in peace with everyone, I can treat my brother better."

Ask:

● **Based on what we've learned from this course and specifically this activity, how is discipleship more than simply a decision?** (It's a way of life; it's a challenge for every day; it's a growth process.)

● **According to Jesus' statements in Matthew 28:16-20, what's our responsibility as disciples?** (To make disciples of others; to preach and teach others.)

Say: **Each day as disciples, we must strive to develop the characteristics Paul speaks about in Romans 12:9-21. But sometimes we fall short in one or more of these areas.**

SIGN ON THE DOTTED LINE

Form pairs. Give pairs each two pieces of paper, pencils, a candle and matches. Have kids look at the characteristics of a disciple from the "Discipleship Lifestyle" handout (p. 41).

Have kids each list on a piece of paper one characteristic they need to improve from the handout list. Then have them each talk with their partner about how they can improve in that area.

Have teenagers each write a statement of commitment to work on developing this characteristic over the coming week. Remind teenagers this is a time for serious reflection. Then have them each fold their paper so the top and bottom edges overlap in the middle of the paper. Have them each silently light the candle and drip wax over the visible edge to seal their paper closed. Have kids then each sign their name on the front of their paper.

Form a circle. Have teenagers each take a turn silently placing their sealed paper in the center of the circle. While students are still quiet, move into the Closing.

OPTION 1: PRAYER CIRCLE

Have teenagers each take a turn standing in the center of the circle next to the sealed papers. As each person stands in the circle, have the rest of the teenagers pray silently for him or her. You might have teenagers in the circle reach out and touch the person in the center as they pray. Have teenagers each pick up one paper—other than their own—from the circle. Then have them each write on the back of the paper why they appreciate the person whose name is on the paper they hold. Ask teenagers to deliver the papers to their owners.

OPTION 2: DISCIPLESHIP SENTENCES

After you read each of the following sentences aloud, encourage each teenager to respond verbally:

● **The hardest thing about being a true disciple is . . .**
● **The best thing about being a true disciple is . . .**

Have kids collect their papers from the center of the circle. Form groups of no more than four. Have teenagers in each group tell what discipleship quality they appreciate about the other people in their group. Then have groups pray together. Encourage teenagers to take their commitment papers home to remind them to seek the discipleship lifestyle each day.

If You Still Have Time . . .

Course Reflection—Form a circle. Ask students to reflect on the past four lessons. Have them take turns completing the following sentences:

● Something I learned in this course was . . .
● If I could tell my friends about this course, I'd say . . .
● Something I'll do differently because of this course is . . .

JOB DESCRIPTION

Complete this form to create a job description for disciples. Use the information from the previous three lessons and any other insights you might have on what it means to be a disciple.

I. Name of position: **Disciple**

II. Qualifications for the job:

1. _____   4. _____

2. _____   5. _____

3. _____   6. _____

III. Specific duties:

1. _____

2. _____

3. _____

IV. Benefits of the job:

1. _____   4. _____

2. _____   5. _____

3. _____   6. _____

V. Risks involved in the job:

1. _____   4. _____

2. _____   5. _____

3. _____   6. _____

Discipleship Lifestyle

For each item, indicate how easy or difficult it is for you to live out this discipleship characteristic by marking the appropriate box. Then in your group discuss the questions at the bottom of the page.

	Easy	A struggle sometimes	Difficult
1. Love others sincerely.	☐	☐	☐
2. Hate what is evil.	☐	☐	☐
3. Hold on to what is good and pure.	☐	☐	☐
4. Be devoted to each other with love.	☐	☐	☐
5. Honor others above yourself.	☐	☐	☐
6. Keep your spiritual enthusiasm.	☐	☐	☐
7. Be joyful and have hope for the future.	☐	☐	☐
8. Be patient.	☐	☐	☐
9. Pray faithfully.	☐	☐	☐
10. Share with people in need.	☐	☐	☐
11. Practice hospitality.	☐	☐	☐
12. Pray for those who persecute me.	☐	☐	☐
13. Empathize with others.	☐	☐	☐
14. Spend time with the "unloved" people.	☐	☐	☐
15. Don't be conceited.	☐	☐	☐
16. Don't seek revenge.	☐	☐	☐
17. Try to live in peace with everyone.	☐	☐	☐
18. Overcome evil with good.	☐	☐	☐

● Which characteristics are most important? Place a star next to each of the three most-important characteristics. Talk about these in your group.

● How can you develop these characteristics?

● Look at the boxes you've checked. How do you feel about your answers? What can you do to improve your answers?

Table Talk

To the Parent: This month we've been studying Christian discipleship at church. Please take a few minutes to talk with your senior higher about this topic. Use this sheet to spark discussion about the topic.

Complete the following sentences.

Parent

- On a scale of 1 to 10 my spiritual life as a senior higher was . . .

- The person who had the most influence on me spiritually was . . .

- The event that shaped my spiritual life most was . . .

- The time in my life when I was most serious spiritually was . . .

- My spiritual life today is . . .

Senior higher

- On a scale of 1 to 10 I'd rate my spiritual life now as . . .

- The person who influences my spiritual life the most is . . .

- The thing I like most about being a Christian is . . .

- The thing that scares me most about being a Christian is . . .

Parent and senior higher

Discuss what it means to live a discipleship lifestyle.

Talk together about the ups and downs in a spiritual journey and how you might help each other develop a discipleship lifestyle.

Then complete the following sentences:

- The things that help me stay close to God are . . .

- The things that pull me away from God are . . .

- It's not easy being a disciple when . . .

- One thing that could help our family spiritually is . . .

Pray together that God will make better disciples of each family member.

BONUS IDEAS

Secret Disciple—Have kids read about Joseph of Arimathea, the first "Secret Disciple" (John 19:38; Matthew 27:57-61; Mark 15:43-47; and Luke 23:50-53). Discuss why he may have been reluctant to "come out of the closet" as a Christian, and why he eventually felt he had to do it. Then have kids tell about times when they felt like Joseph of Arimathea.

Parent Survey—Help students develop a survey of parents' discipleship commitment during their teenage years.

Ask questions such as:

● When you were a teenager, what most held you back from being a committed follower of Jesus?

● What helped you most?

● How did your parents help you develop a discipleship commitment?

Have teenagers survey parents, compile the results and discuss them. Send the survey results to your denominational headquarters or publish them in a regional newsletter.

Play It Up—Have teenagers develop and perform a play for the entire church based on the life of the disciples. Study each disciple, then help students write a short play for each.

Check out the following resources for good information on the disciples: *The Great Physician* by G. Campbell Morgan (Revell) and *All the Apostles of the Bible* by Herbert Lockyer (Zondervan).

Cost and Benefits Board—Develop a bulletin board display. Title one-half of the display "The Cost of Discipleship." Have teenagers create fake price-tags and list on them the "cost" of discipleship based on the following scriptures: Luke 14:26-33 and 2 Corinthians 11:23-30.

Then have them title the other half of the display "Discipleship: Worth the Cost." Have teenagers make this half of the display look like a magazine ad, listing benefits of discipleship and challenging people to "buy into" the discipleship lifestyle.

Wanted Posters—Create "Wanted" posters for each of the original disciples. For each disciple, include information such as: name, what he was known for, when last seen and other unique qualities. Then gather school photos of each of your students and create "Wanted" posters for them using a similar format.

Post all of the "Wanted" posters in a prominent place in your church.

MEETINGS AND MORE

BONUS SCRIPTURES

The lessons focus on a select few scripture passages, but if you'd like to incorporate more Bible readings into the lessons, here are our suggestions:

● Isaiah 53:1-6 (We have all made mistakes.)

● John 13:34-35 (Love one another as God Loves us.)

● Romans 1:16-17 (Don't be ashamed of he gospel.)

● 2 Corinthians 5:16-21 (If we're in Christ, we're new creations.)

● Colossians 3:17 (Whatever we say or do, do it in Jesus' name.)

● Hebrews 10:19-25 (Consider how to encourage each other toward love and good deeds.)

Scavenger Hunt—Use the "Disciple Scavenger Hunt" handout (p. 45) to plan a fun scavenger hunt for your students. Have them form teams and search for the items on the list. Award a prize for the team that returns with the most items in one hour. Be sure to have kids return important items to owners after the activity.

Table Talk—Use the "Table Talk" handout (p. 42) as the basis for discussion between mixed groups of parents and teenagers. Plan for a low-pressure time of sharing on discipleship.

Include games and crowdbreakers as well as serious time to discuss what it means to be a disciple in today's society. For crowdbreaker ideas, check out *Quick Games and Crowdbreakers for Youth Groups* (Group Books).

RETREAT IDEA

Thirteenth Disciple Retreat—Plan a retreat around the theme of "The 13th Disciple." Advertise the retreat as a training camp for disciples.

At the end of the retreat, have an awards ceremony to honor each teenager for a special discipleship characteristic. Also award the coveted "13th Disciple" award to each teenager. Have teenagers create a closing worship service based on the challenge of discipleship.

PARTY PLEASER

Worth It Party—Plan an entire party around the theme "It's Tough, But It's Worth It" about the challenge of discipleship. Serve food that takes work to make or eat, such as unshelled Brazil nuts, clams or fondue. Have teenagers bake bread, cookies or doughnuts.

Arrange big boxes and tables to form a difficult maze for kids to crawl through to get to the party. Play games that are difficult but fun to participate in, such as tossing pingpong balls into small cups across the room. Talk about how sometimes the better things in life take effort.

DISCIPLE SCAVENGER HUNT

Find the following items. Only one item may be taken from
any one house. Have the owner of the item sign in the space provided.

Disciple	Item to Find	Owner's Signature
Matthew (Matthew 9:9-12)	A state or federal tax form	_____
Peter (Matthew 4:18-20)	A fishing rod	_____
Judas (Matthew 26:14-16)	30 dimes	_____
James (Matthew 4:21-22)	A toy boat	_____
Nathanael (John 1:45-51)	A Fig Newton cookie	_____
Andrew (Matthew 14:15-18)	Five slices of bread and a can of sardines	_____
Thomas (John 20:24-28)	Something people would doubt where you got it	_____
John (Luke 22:7-13)	A jar filled with water	_____

CURRICULUM REORDER—TOP PRIORITY

Order now to prepare for your upcoming Sunday school classes, youth ministry meetings, and weekend retreats! Each book includes all teacher and student materials—plus photocopiable handouts—for any size class...for just $8.99 each!

FOR SENIOR HIGH:

1 & 2 Corinthians: Christian Discipleship, ISBN 1-55945-230-7

Angels, Demons, Miracles & Prayer, ISBN 1-55945-235-8

Changing the World, ISBN 1-55945-236-6

Christians in a Non-Christian World, ISBN 1-55945-224-2

Christlike Leadership, ISBN 1-55945-231-5

Communicating With Friends, ISBN 1-55945-228-5

Counterfeit Religions, ISBN 1-55945-207-2

Dating Decisions, ISBN 1-55945-215-3

Dealing With Life's Pressures, ISBN 1-55945-232-3

Deciphering Jesus' Parables, ISBN 1-55945-237-4

Exodus: Following God, ISBN 1-55945-226-9

Exploring Ethical Issues, ISBN 1-55945-225-0

Faith for Tough Times, ISBN 1-55945-216-1

Forgiveness, ISBN 1-55945-223-4

Getting Along With Parents, ISBN 1-55945-202-1

Getting Along With Your Family, ISBN 1-55945-233-1

The Gospel of John: Jesus' Teachings, ISBN 1-55945-208-0

Hazardous to Your Health: AIDS, Steroids & Eating Disorders, ISBN 1-55945-200-5

Is Marriage in Your Future?, ISBN 1-55945-203-X

Jesus' Death & Resurrection, ISBN 1-55945-211-0

The Joy of Serving, ISBN 1-55945-210-2

Knowing God's Will, ISBN 1-55945-205-6

Life After High School, ISBN 1-55945-220-X

Making Good Decisions, ISBN 1-55945-209-9

Money: A Christian Perspective, ISBN 1-55945-212-9

Movies, Music, TV & Me, ISBN 1-55945-213-7

Overcoming Insecurities, ISBN 1-55945-221-8

Psalms, ISBN 1-55945-234-X

Real People, Real Faith: Amy Grant, Joni Eareckson Tada, Dave Dravecky, Terry Anderson, ISBN 1-55945-238-2

Responding to Injustice, ISBN 1-55945-214-5

Revelation, ISBN 1-55945-229-3

School Struggles, ISBN 1-55945-201-3

Sex: A Christian Perspective, ISBN 1-55945-206-4

Today's Lessons From Yesterday's Prophets, ISBN 1-55945-227-7

Turning Depression Upside Down, ISBN 1-55945-135-1

What Is the Church?, ISBN 1-55945-222-6

Who Is God?, ISBN 1-55945-218-8

Who Is Jesus?, ISBN 1-55945-219-6

Who Is the Holy Spirit?, ISBN 1-55945-217-X

Your Life as a Disciple, ISBN 1-55945-204-8

FOR JUNIOR HIGH/MIDDLE SCHOOL:

Accepting Others: Beyond Barriers & Stereotypes, ISBN 1-55945-126-2

Advice to Young Christians: Exploring Paul's Letters, ISBN 1-55945-146-7

Applying the Bible to Life, ISBN 1-55945-116-5

Becoming Responsible, ISBN 1-55945-109-2

Bible Heroes: Joseph, Esther, Mary & Peter, ISBN 1-55945-137-8

Boosting Self-Esteem, ISBN 1-55945-100-9

Building Better Friendships, ISBN 1-55945-138-6

Can Christians Have Fun?, ISBN 1-55945-134-3

Caring for God's Creation, ISBN 1-55945-121-1

Christmas: A Fresh Look, ISBN 1-55945-124-6

Competition, ISBN 1-55945-133-5

Dealing With Death, ISBN 1-55945-112-2

Dealing With Disappointment, ISBN 1-55945-139-4

Doing Your Best, ISBN 1-55945-142-4

Drugs & Drinking, ISBN 1-55945-118-1

Evil and the Occult, ISBN 1-55945-102-5

Genesis: The Beginnings, ISBN 1-55945-111-4

Guys & Girls: Understanding Each Other, ISBN 1-55945-110-6

Handling Conflict, ISBN 1-55945-125-4

Heaven & Hell, ISBN 1-55945-131-9

Is God Unfair?, ISBN 1-55945-108-4

Love or Infatuation?, ISBN 1-55945-128-9

Making Parents Proud, ISBN 1-55945-107-6

Making the Most of School, ISBN 1-55945-113-0

Materialism, ISBN 1-55945-130-0

The Miracle of Easter, ISBN 1-55945-143-2

Miracles!, ISBN 1-55945-117-3

Peace & War, ISBN 1-55945-123-8

Peer Pressure, ISBN 1-55945-103-3

Prayer, ISBN 1-55945-104-1

Reaching Out to a Hurting World, ISBN 1-55945-140-8

Sermon on the Mount, ISBN 1-55945-129-7

Suicide: The Silent Epidemic, ISBN 1-55945-145-9

Telling Your Friends About Christ, ISBN 1-55945-114-9

The Ten Commandments, ISBN 1-55945-127-0

Today's Faith Heroes: Madeline Manning Mims, Michael W. Smith, Mother Teresa, Bruce Olson, ISBN 1-55945-141-6

Today's Media: Choosing Wisely, ISBN 1-55945-144-0

Today's Music: Good or Bad?, ISBN 1-55945-101-7

What Is God's Purpose for Me?, ISBN 1-55945-132-7

What's a Christian?, ISBN 1-55945-105-X

Order today from your local Christian bookstore, or write: Group Publishing, Box 485, Loveland, CO 80539. For mail orders, please add postage/handling of $4 for orders up to $15, $5 for orders of $15.01+. Colorado residents add 3% sales tax.

BRING THE BIBLE TO LIFE FOR YOUR 5TH- AND 6TH-GRADERS WITH GROUP'S *HANDS-ON BIBLE CURRICULUM*®

Energize your kids with Active Learning!

Group's **Hands-On Bible Curriculum** will help you teach the Bible in a radical new way. It's based on Active Learning—the same teaching method Jesus used.

Research shows that we retain less than 10% of what we hear or read. *But we remember up to 90% of what we experience.* Your 5th- and 6th-graders will experience spiritual lessons and learn to apply them to their daily lives! And—they'll go home remembering what they've learned.

In each lesson, students will participate in exciting and memorable learning experiences using fascinating gadgets and gizmos you've not seen with any other curriculum. Your 5th- and 6th-graders will discover biblical truths and <u>remember</u> what they learn—because they're <u>doing</u> instead of just listening.

You'll save time and money too!

While students are learning more, you'll be working less—simply follow the quick and easy instructions in the Teachers Guide. You'll get tons of material for an energy-packed 35- to 60-minute lesson. And, if you have extra time, there's an arsenal of Bonus Ideas and Time Stuffers to keep kids occupied—and learning! Plus, you'll SAVE BIG over other curriculum programs that require you to buy expensive separate student books—all student handouts in Group's **Hands-On Bible Curriculum** are photocopiable!

In addition to the easy-to-use Teachers Guide, you'll get all the essential teaching materials you need in a ready-to-use Learning Lab®. No more running from store to store hunting for lesson materials—all the active-learning tools you need to teach 13 exciting Bible lessons to any size class are provided for you in the Learning Lab.

Challenging topics every 13 weeks keep your kids coming back!

Group's **Hands-On Bible Curriculum** covers topics that matter to your kids and teaches them the Bible with integrity. Every quarter you'll explore three meaningful Bible-based subjects. Switching topics every month keeps your 5th- and 6th-graders enthused and coming back for more. The full two-year program will help your kids...

• make God-pleasing decisions,
• recognize their God-given potential, and
• seek to grow as Christians.

Take the boredom out of Sunday school, children's church, and youth group for your 5th- and 6th-graders. Make your job easier and more rewarding with no-fail lessons that are ready in a flash. Order Group's **Hands-On Bible Curriculum** for your 5th- and 6th-graders today.